Becoming Just

"S T Kimbrough Jr. raises a myriad of critically poignant questions about justice issues confronting the world, including our own paradigmatic status on democracy and rights. He does not offer platitudes, but stresses an ongoing need for repentance, and a steady course guaranteeing freedom and rights: love kindness, do justice, so it rolls down like water and an ever-flowing river; this is indeed to walk humbly with our Lord."

—**CHARLES AMJAD-ALI**, Martin Luther King Jr. Professor of Justice and Christian Community (Emeritus) at Luther Seminary

"The many verses in S T Kimbrough Jr.'s *Becoming Just* speak to me. They remind me there is no 'just' for justice. Not really. For justice is more than *just* race, or *just* gender, or *just* creed, or *just* nationality, or *just* us. Becoming just is a constant quest for decency to all, a concerted push for equality, an evolution within ourselves and in the parts we play to the world."

—**JOHN ARCHIBALD**, 2018 Pulitzer Prize winner in Commentary

"The foreword to S T Kimbrough Jr.'s new book of poems, *Becoming Just*, opens with Martin Luther King's words, 'The arc of the moral universe is long, but it bends towards justice.' These poems further the bending of that arc in a fascinating and challenging way. The poems largely focus on personal, societal, and governmental injustices, and the reader is left with the challenge of 'What can I do to right these injustices?'"

—**WILLIAM N. CLARK**, attorney

Becoming Just

*Poems that Explore Commitment
to Justice for All*

S T Kimbrough, Jr.

Foreword by Jackson W. Carroll

RESOURCE *Publications* · Eugene, Oregon

BECOMING JUST
Poems that Explore Commitment to Justice for All

Resource Publications
An Imprint of Wipf and Stock Publishers
199 W. 8th Ave., Suite 3
Eugene, OR 97401

www.wipfandstock.com

PAPERBACK ISBN: 978-1-6667-5033-1
HARDCOVER ISBN: 978-1-6667-5034-8
EBOOK ISBN: 978-1-6667-5035-5

08/23/22

Contents

Foreword

THE ARC OF THE universe is long, but bends toward justice. These words,[1] often quoted by Dr. Martin Luther King, Jr., reflect the conviction that enabled him to persevere in the face of fierce opposition and abuse. They are a fitting way to introduce this collection of poems by S T Kimbrough, Jr., as he gives vivid expression to the myriad forms that both injustice and justice take in today's moral universe and the ways they challenge us to bend with it toward justice.Justice, as Kimbrough notes in his Introduction, is complex, with multiple dimensions to which he gives expression in the various sections of the book. Over the centuries, philosophers, theologians, social scientists, and many others have debated the meaning and origin of our ideas and ideals of justice: Are they divinely given commandments? Are they derived from natural law? Are they simply reflections of long-established communal norms institutionalized as common law? Or are they expressions of human rationality? Whatever their origin, the core of their concern, as Kimbrough says, is "how can fairness for all and everything be achieved?"This includes fairness at the personal, societal, national, and global levels, each with its own challenges in our complex and changing world. So what does it mean to act justly so that fairness can be achieved? While there are numerous ways of answering this question, for Christians, the clearest answer is surely Jesus' commandment to love God and our neighbors as ourselves[2]—neighbors who include, among others, the poor, the

---

1. The quotation was originally in a published sermon by the prominent abolitionist Unitarian minister, Theodore Parker, in 1853.

2. This answer for Christians is shared, as Kimbrough notes, by our sisters

suffering, the hungry, the homeless, migrant children separated from their parents at our borders, those who have been displaced by wars, land grabs, or natural disasters. And what does it mean to respond in love in these diverse and difficult circumstances? One response would be to ask, as some do, "What would Jesus do?" ("WWJD?").[3] In some situations, the answer may be fairly obvious, as it seems to have been to the Samaritan in Jesus' parable, but not to the priest and lawyer who, unlike the Samaritan, passed by the wounded man without stopping to help. Often, however, the challenges we face to act justly are not so straightforward—as is true for most of those Kimbrough addresses in his poems—making it difficult for us to see clearly how to respond in love, and not have to think that asking "WWJD?" will provide an adequate or realistic answer. Furthermore, we are frequently held back from seeing and responding in love by self-interest, or by our unspoken and often unrecognized biases that reflect our race, ethnicity, gender, or social class, as was the case with the priest and lawyer in the Samaritan parable. Racism and belief in white supremacy die hard and continue to leave Black Americans suffering from myriad injustices despite growing anti-racist efforts to address them. Antisemitism also continues to rear its ugly head both in the U. S. and elsewhere; yet, many Jews nevertheless support harsh, unjust Israeli policies and practices that oppress and bring great suffering to their Palestinian neighbors.

It also exceedingly difficult for groups to act solely and purely in love at the social, national, or global level. Cross-pressures and multiple claims and counter claims by competing interests make it nearly impossible to discern what love requires in many situations. Is there a single common good to be sought? Or are there competing or conflicting goods, each with its own idea of what a just and loving response might be? In the conflict raging in the Ukraine, as

---

and brothers in the other Abrahamic faiths, Judaism and Islam.

3. Asking WWJD? became a frequent question in recent popular religious culture, but it was given full expression over a century ago in the bestselling 1897 novel, *In His Steps*, by Charles M. Sheldon, a Congregational pastor and leader in the Social Gospel Movement.

Foreword

I write this Foreword, NATO's resistance to a "no-fly zone" over Ukraine—which Ukrainian leaders view as a common good that would likely save many lives—is based on NATO leaders' fear of starting World War III—what these leaders believe to be the common good for Europe and the United States. Or, as Kimbrough's poems in the section on Apartheid and Justice make clear, U. S. support for Palestinians, and especially for residents of Gaza, runs headlong into opposition from groups in the United States with strong pro-Zionist sentiments, and who resist any assistance to the Palestinian cause. In contrast, Gazans look at the considerable U. S. support currently being given to Ukraine and wonder why the often-promised U. S. aid to them has been so limited and slow in coming, or has failed to come at all. Yes, it is often difficult to know what love demands. The point of the provocative poems in this book, however, is not that we should throw up our hands in despair and do nothing. Instead, they help us to remember that, though long and fraught with obstacles, the arc of the moral universe does bend towards justice. Difficult as it may be to know how to respond or to find the will to respond, God does not let us off the hook. But God also helps us to bend with the moral universe as we seek to become just, as the book's title suggests.

Jackson W. Carroll
Williams Distinguished Professor *Emeritus*
of Religion and Society
The Divinity School, Duke University

Introduction

THE CONCEPT OF JUSTICE has multiple dimensions depending on language, personal and social context, including ethnic, cultural, and religious perspectives. The burning question remains—How can fairness for all and everything be achieved? Is one to live by the rules of the ten commandments of Hebrew scripture, or by Muslim *shariya*, or other cultural, ethnic, and religious laws? History reveals the plethora of tribal laws and customs by which members have been expected to live. The *lex talionis*, an eye for an eye and a tooth for a tooth, is a perspective that still has its adherents in many societies and cultures. The nations of the world exercise specific judgments for what is just by establishing laws that regulate human behavior. As diligently as legislators and governmental leaders may attempt to create laws that are to be applied justly to all, they often fail, for legal intent and legal application are not always congruent.

The poems in this collection are constantly asking—How can we become just people? This is no simple matter. Many raise overtly or subtly the question—What is human justice? (Section 1) Is there a justice that is equal and/or appropriate for all of human beings?

> Become just, as you do just acts
> and never try to shirk the facts,
> for justice must have advocates
> of truth which justice celebrates.
> Will justice always be the same
> for each occurrence one can name?
> Quite sadly history reveals
> that what's called justice oft conceals

a plethora of unjust acts
that craftily distorts the facts.

There is certainly "no size fits all" when it comes to human justice, for we are all human beings.

In this all humans are alike:
they live awhile, then death will strike.

They may not always think the same,
but one the other shouldn't defame.

And while they're living they should try
the lives of all to dignify!

Along with the question of justice for all, there is the question of personal justice (Section 2). Beyond perspectives of a just society in which all are to be treated justly is the question of personal justice. How can an individual in action, speech, and behavior be a just individual? How does one think of oneself as just in one's interaction with others?

Oft Good Samaritans are rare,
the folk who think of others first,
whose lives exude a sense of care
with kindness daily interspersed.

Is it possible to be someone who thinks of others first? Is this necessary? It depends on what kind of just society one wishes to shape. How the individual behaves is of vital importance. By what standard(s) does one know what to do?

But they must stop right where they are
and see the suffering in need.
Ignore no one, though near or far,
and be the help for which they plead.

Being human means that we are aware that there is a humanness in all that must be respected or there can be no justice whatsoever.

Introduction

All who were once embryos join
the human race through the wonder of birth,
when, unless deprived of health,
all have the capacity to live and love.
To be truly human means to honor and
foster this capacity in *every* person.

When it comes to the question of justice, I think so often
of children (Section 3), and the injustices done to them through
the ages. Perhaps this is because my wife and I had four sons
and nine grandchildren. And now there are eight great grand-
children. Children give us new hope. They are a reservoir of un-
fulfilled dreams. They possess potential to be realized and talent
and skills to be developed. The death of a child means that none
of this can come to fruition.

Not only the parents or guardians, if there are any, bear the
responsibility for the growth and development of a child. Society
shares this responsibility. It may deny a child the opportunity of
fulfillment. It may shortchange educational options. It may reject
the idea that there is social responsibility for every child, which
cannot be obviated without the destruction of society itself.

These poems address what children may or may not learn
from adults and their peers. They speak of the uniqueness of every
child and at times of society's denial of its responsibility. They ad-
dress the privileged and the underprivileged child. They describe
the terror of war and its creation of orphans. However, they also
speak of hope and the uniqueness of every child.

It matters not culture or creed,
a Christian, Moslem, Jew,
each child from hatred must be freed
to live, to self be true.

Many contexts today raise the question of how refugee chil-
dren are to be treated. What if they have been orphaned by war
or domestic gun violence? Does society have no responsibility
for them?

For children, who are refugees
and find themselves detained,
are damaged slowly by degrees,
their happiness restrained.

They've lost their parents in their flight,
or guards took them away.
Without their touch it's fright on fright!
Who can this fear allay?

The distinguished statesman Frederick Douglass is reported to have said: "It is easier to build strong children than to repair broken men."

It's better to build children strong,
with boldness Douglass claims,
than to repair all of your wrong
and all their broken aims.

Are there aspects of justice framed by society (Section 4) that are determined more by human response than legal definition? How do we wish to live in a society—isolated, completely independent, self-centered? Living in a society implies association, relating to others in some manner. How do we wish to relate to others? Shall we heed these words?

Care for the next, the next is near,
let neighbor love be paramount!
Bold honesty, respect revere,
all hatred, prejudice discount!

The Corona Virus pandemic has stressed throughout the world the importance of civility and hospitality. Both remind us of our responsibility to others. Some wish blindly to assert their personal right(s) above all others in the following manner:

"No mask, no vaccine, that's my right.
I want them both out of my sight."
But you can be a carrier,
that breaks down every barrier.
To claim a "right" that is a crime
could wind up murd'ring in due time.

There is a need to ask oneself—How do I wish to be seen by others?

> If others see in us a friend,
>   someone who's filled with care,
> our lives in friendship soon will blend:
>   the human race's dare!

When one thinks of the heritage of Jim Crow laws in the southern United States and realizes that there are hundreds of years of injustice to overcome, one quickly grasps that this is a mandate of every generation. The injustices created by such laws have lingered and lingered in a variety of ways that can be rectified only by a society itself. An African American pastor-poet, Charles Albert Tindley (1851–1933), who lived in the first part of the twentieth century, wrote a hymn titled "I'll overcome some day" that would be transformed into "We shall overcome" during the Civil Rights Movement.

> The people soon transformed the song
>   to "We shall overcome."
> They sang it nights and all day long
>   that Jim Crow would succumb,
>
> succumb to justice and just laws,
>   minorities protect,
> for Black Lives Matter's a just cause,
>   no person may neglect.

Tindley's "I" was transformed to "we," for this is a corporate, societal venture, which "no person may neglect."

An essential aspect of "societal justice" is "governmental justice" (Section 5). How will the governments under which we live, initiate and execute just rule and governance for all citizens? Of course, there are diverse forms of government which institute laws to oversee what is "seen" as just and justice. Totalitarian governments leave little responsibility, if at all, to the people to determine what is just. In such contexts the citizens serve the state, and its rulers without accountability demonstrate their lust for power.

> Why humans have a lust for power
> is not a mystery,
> since human history is dour,
> and filled with misery.
>
> . . .
>
> The evil that goes on today
> comes from abusive power,
> attempts vast cultures to betray,
> their land, lives to devour.

Though I am a citizen of the world, I write as an American who learned as a child the "Pledge of Allegiance" to the US flag, which ends with the powerful line, "with liberty and justice for all." However, I grew up in the segregated South, attended segregated schools, and rode buses and street cars that put African Americans in the back.

> Where's "Liberty . . . justice for all"—
> the last phrase that our forebears wrote?
> Do they express our grave downfall?
> Should we refuse these words to quote?

Of course, we need to hold on to this dream, but also to realize our country's failure in achieving such justice. We hear politicians, regardless of party affiliation, conclude speech after speech with "God bless America." If we weigh the wrong and the right America has done in its history, do we have reason to believe God will bless America any more than another nation?

> Of monuments to Lincoln, King
> we stalwartly are proud,
> but native nations all would sing
> if here stood Chief Red Cloud.
>
> The idea of the USA
> did not begin with ease,
> for freedom, justice went astray,
> which brings us to our knees.

It is difficult for present-day generations to repent for the wrongs of their forebears. Yet generations of living Native

Americans and African Americans, whose parents fought for freedom against the unjust Nazi war machine, know that they do not enjoy the freedom for which their parents fought.

> Although we all for freedom fought
> regardless of our race,
> the racism many were taught,
> is still easy to trace.

America now experiences extreme polarization among its citizens. There has not only been the daunting shadow of insurrection at the nation's capital, there are threats to one of the most precious rights US citizens have, namely, the right to vote and freely express one's opinion in the choice of those who represent the public and create the laws by which the people will be governed.

> This precious right some would deny
> to those who live in poverty,
> or race can be the reason why;
> white-power would with this agree.

> All human beings have the right
> to vote on their own destiny.
> Those who reject this are a blight,
> committing a gross felony!

There is desperate need to reclaim democracy if America is to survive as a nation.

> Reclaim democracy, speak truth:
> example be for all our youth.
> Reclaim democracy, act just;
> eliminate hate and distrust.
> Reclaim democracy, don't lie,
> all falsehoods and all theft decry.
> Reclaim democracy and make
> accountable every mistake.
> Reclaim democracy, admit
> the wrongs that you, others commit.
> Reclaim democracy, defy—
> all prejudices bid goodbye.

Reclaim democracy, be true:
accept the LGBTQ.
. . .
Reclaim democracy and trust
that citizens learn to be just!

Section 6 is titled "Apartheid and Justice" and is essentially a lyrical case study of apartheid injustice that the US government has supported in two primary ways: (1) by refusing to name the wrong for what it is, namely, apartheid injustice. While the US strongly supported the breakup of the apartheid system in South Africa, albeit somewhat late, it has refused to confront and oppose apartheid injustice in Israel in like fashion. (2) It has supported apartheid injustice with grants of billions dollars to the state of Israel, whose acts against the Palestinians are contrary to the ethics and moral principles for which the US says it stands, i.e. the ongoing confiscation of Palestinian land, the nonstop building of settlements on Palestinian land, the imprisonment of Palestinians without charges, inequitable destruction of Palestinian homes, the denial of equal rights to Palestinian inhabitants of Israel, etc. Interestingly, Vladimir Putin's authorization of the destruction of civilians' dwellings in Ukraine is now being challenged as a war crime. What of Israel's destruction of Palestinians' dwellings?

Israel makes the bold claim of being a democracy. Yes, many of us in America acknowledge that our own democracy has failed in many ways and has the ongoing need of recovering the principles of justice and equality. Americans know well the meaning of ethnic cleansing in their own land.

Thus ethnic cleansing's kept alive
in Middle Eastern "Holy Land."
For purity Israelis strive
as Palestinians are banned
from homes in East Jerusalem
where forefathers before them lived.
And home by home they now condemn
as Palestinians are deceived.

A Middle East "democracy"
  the nation Israel claims to be.
But it is sheer hypocrisy
  to honor exclusivity.
Democracy honors the whole,
  where all are equal in the state,
led by majority control.
  In Israel is it now too late?

The poems in this little volume make no claim at successful resolutions to the issues raised. They do point toward the ongoing need of repentance for wrongs done, and for steering a steady course to guarantee the rights of freedom and justice for all people.

Section 1

Human Justice

1. Becoming Just

Become just, as you do just acts
and never try to shirk the facts,
for justice must have advocates
of truth which justice celebrates.
Will justice always be the same
for each occurrence one can name?
Quite sadly history reveals
that what's called justice oft conceals
a plethora of unjust acts
that craftily distorts the facts.
The color of one's skin may be
what hinders justice frequently,
or gender may change someone's views
and prejudices in the news.
Become just, as you do just acts
and never try to shirk the facts.

2. The Humane Test

Some think they're right, and others wrong,
about whatever comes along.
They're desperate that others hear
their prejudices filled with fear.
They warn against aid to the weak,
which makes the wealthy's future bleak.
While they rage on and criticize
another Covid patient dies.
Though vaccine aid was on the way,
some politicians caused delay.
While some of them would prove their case,
must one for more infections brace?
But if they know that they are right,
they care not who dies day or night.
What does it take to be humane?
Refuse to act as if insane,
for it's insane to let folks die,
Coronavirus facts deny.
To compromise is not a curse,
intransigence is much, much worse.
Subdue your pride and save a soul,
don't add to opposition's toll;
its toll of death one can reduce.
It's time to seal a humane truce.
A humane truce thinks first of those
whom one must not choose to oppose.
It helps the weak, the poor, the strong.
It favors all amid the throng

of people living on a street,
or rural farmers that you meet.
Forget you think that you know best,
and you'll have passed the humane test.

3. Dignity

Who will decide what matters most?
Who has the right of self to boast?

Do some have rights, others do not?
Whence come the rights that you have got?

If you have light or darkened skin,
is color then a deadly sin?

All human beings are alike;
they live awhile, then death will strike.

They may not always think the same,
but others they should not defame.

And while they're living they should try
the lives of all to dignify!

4. Truth, Honesty, Respect

Truth, honesty, respect for all,
    my parents taught all three,
but other voices seem to call,
    and all three seem to flee.

They eagerly flee with discourse
    of politicians, friends.
Is there at hand some joint resource
    that this charade upends?

Oh yes, there is a joint resource:
    it is the human race!
It's you and me, not some new course,
    but is there left a trace?

Is there a trace of self-respect
    left midst all humankind
by which this tragedy is checked
    in every human mind?

The human mind alone's the hope
    but difficult to sway,
to stop the single-minded trope:
    "My way's the only way."

This biased, single-minded trope
    destroys truth and respect.
There is no single way to cope,
    no single truth effect.

But if today there is no quest
    these three anew to find,
then humankind becomes a jest:
    to chaos is resigned!

5. Death-Lust

What reasons can a human give
why other humans should not live?
Attempts of some to justify
gross evil acts will mystify.
One takes a life and courts decide
the sentence "death," which must abide.
When ethnic cleansing comes in view,
one thinks of Holocaust, the Jew.
But ethnic cleansing comes to pass
on Palestinians *en masse*.
And what of the Armenian purge
and white supremacy's new surge?
There's Russia's purging of Ukraine
with human slaughter that's insane?
What motivates this strange death-lust?
How can one think that it is just?

6. Human Magic

There's magic waiting to be found
    in words, in smiles, in phrases,
We learn that simple things astound,
    the unforeseen amazes.

Oh yes, there's magic in our speech,
    there's magic in our actions.
Do we believe we magic teach
    in spite of all distractions?

Suppose that we all ethnic slurs
    reject when we are speaking,
we'll show our speech respect prefers,
    respect all should be seeking.

There is a magic that we own,
    the magic shared with others.
Love's magic should leave none alone,
    love's magic discord smothers.

Is magic from some netherworld
    that leaves no earthly traces,
or from some secret place unfurled
    beyond all time and places?

My friends, magicians all are we,
    for magic we're creating.
What magic can folk hope to see?
    Our magic they're awaiting!

7. Sacredness

If life that is a sacred trust,
misguided souls see with disgust,
if sacredness they disregard
and tend its values to discard,
the innocence of a newborn
can quickly from its life be shorn.
If sacredness comes with each birth,
there's sacredness throughout the earth.
What then does sacred really mean?—
Each life as precious must be seen!
And when you violate this trust,
your life is ashes, dust to dust!

8. To Be Born

In love a child should be conceived;
    there's no regard to race or creed.
Though hope is happily believed,
    vile prejudice can sow its seed.

If red, black, yellow, brown the skin,
    the child may suffer bias, hate.
How strange, for humans are all kin!
    How long for justice must they wait?

All children are conceived alike:
    a female egg joins with male sperm.
But bias after birth may strike,
    where prejudice stands harsh and firm.

All people come from love's great gift,
    creation's multi-colored range.
Our human hues aren't for a rift;
    they're for our beauty to exchange.

So let creation's wonders mark
    the beauty, unity, and hope,
that we together then may spark
    in human love a broadened scope.

9. Human Will

Is there a time we're without war
    and people struggling to survive,
when refugees aren't at our door
    with hope somehow they'll stay alive?

It seems our constant hope is peace,
    but our peace respites don't last long,
when governments use the police
    to create, foster civil wrong.

Control each loud opposing voice
    that cries out "Justice is for all!"
Control the right to make a choice
    and make the opposition fall.

Yet history does the fact reveal:
    control of others will not last.
The human will is strong as steel
    and perseveres, ill will outlasts.

While thousands die at tyrants' hands
    somewhere, somehow justice breaks through,
and those oppressed in many lands
    find bold new ways hope to pursue.

Though human loss is drastic, grave,
    as humans others dare to kill,
one thing alone can humans save,
    the brave, God-given human will.

10. Forgotten Mercy

If Victor Hugo counseled well:
that "Being good is easy,
what's difficult is being just,"
when lawyers' acts are sleazy.

"If justice we do not maintain,"
claimed painter Francis Bacon,
then "us maintain, justice will not!"
It's time that we awaken!

"Justice delayed, justice denied,"
so spoke distinguished Gladstone.
Yet, if delayed and if denied,
the truth can never be known!

If Hugo, Gladstone, Bacon all
for suffering millions plead,
why is compassion now so rare,
the world so full of need?

Section 2

Personal Justice

11. Break Bread with Others

The invitation to break bread
    invites you to give thanks for food.
But thanks must also then be said
    for those whom you from food exclude.

Break bread with others and make friends;
    break bread with others and make peace.
Break bread with others, make amends;
    make malice and ill will decrease.

12. Greed

What you may claim is yours, is mine,
    so goes the claim of greed.
If avarice your thoughts confine,
    you'll take more than you need.

The greedy soul is prone to take
    more, more, and even more.
Ev'n if child hunger is at stake,
    the gluttonous ignore.

The avaricious rob the poor,
    leave children without care;
think first of self, that's to be sure,
    make poverty a snare.

The greedy are most sure to reap
    the emptiness they've sown.
There's not a single thing they'll keep,
    for death alone they own!

13. Rare Good Samaritans

Oft Good Samaritans are rare,
    the folk who think of others first,
whose lives exude a sense of care
    with kindness daily interspersed.

They often lend a smile, a hand,
    perhaps warm friendship or a meal.
The point is this: they take a stand
    and try to learn what lost folk feel.

And those who do not have such needs,
    such life issues they do not face,
must learn that they can sow the seeds
    of kindness, goodness, love, and grace.

But they must stop right where they are
    and see the suffering in need.
Ignore no one, though near or far,
    and be the help for which they plead.

14. The Old Revised

An ancient proverb circulates;
distorted, it articulates:
"Do unto others for your good,
and never treat them as you should.
For profit use every device,
just lie and cheat while acting nice."
This is a way of life for some
who to all ethics become numb.

15. The Test of All Mortality

The test of all mortality:
avoid all immorality
and seek a just morality.

In each one's personality
are options for cordiality
and generous hospitality.

Make kindness a normality
and filled with geniality,
plus honest impartiality.

There's so much illegality
and blatant criminality
resulting in brutality.

I long for joviality,
occasional triviality,
and even whimsicality.

I long for commonality
and humankind's plurality.
There is originality!

16. What Will We Give a Child?

I saw a child just yesterday
who wanted eagerly to play,
and yet upon a cot she lay.
Without both legs she could not stand,
her arms outstretched without one hand,
her eyes asked, Do you understand?

Why must wars punish children first?
At least it seems that they are cursed
to be the victims when bombs burst.
It matters not the race or creed,
a child's a child always in need
of love, for love each one will plead.

Give *each* child freely love and care,
though parents are no longer there,
for each of us has love to share.
More easily we love our own,
than injured children we've not known,
yet we rejoice when they are grown.

They need our love just as they are;
they need it whether near or far,
they need not wish upon a star.
Yes, hope we have each child to give,
a hope that we want them to live.
If not, can we ourselves forgive?

17. Who Am I?

The mystery of self alludes.
When do we know ourselves?
And when does this transpire?
At birth, we do not know our names.
Our first words are celebrated
as we become someone,
who relates to others,
though we have long
related with hugs and kisses.
Words become phrases
and phrases become sentences.
Questions and curiosity begin
to define who we are
and who we are becoming.
Think. Do we remember
when we first thought we
were aware of who we are?
Awareness itself is not
self-knowledge, though without it
one scarcely can look within.
How do we know we have a
conscience and consciousness?
Some cognitive skills, it seems,
just happen as we grow and mature
but others are nurtured by
art, music, reading, drawing, memory.
We may not remember when we became
persons, but we were born human beings.
While we are shaped by many forces,

we do not have to be taught that
we are human, for we were so at birth.
Yet with all that forms and informs us:
education, faith, culture, language,
we do have to be taught to be *human,*
for it is much too easy to learn to be
different from others, to cherish likes
and dislikes, for prejudice is home grown.
Perhaps the best measure of self is to ask:
Do I regard *all* persons as human beings?
All who were once embryos join
the human race through the wonder of birth,
when, unless deprived of health,
all have the capacity to live and love.
To be truly human means to honor and
foster this capacity in *every* person.

18. Whom Will You Ask to Share Your Food?

The difference lives of others make
can make you happy, make you ache,
depending on the view you take.
Whom will you ask to share your food?

Do they for good things have the right,
or do you think they are a blight
and better kept well out of sight?
Whom will you ask to share your food?

There is a test that you should try,
that you may to yourself apply:
to eat with them, do you ask why?
Whom will you ask to share your food?

The key is: learn to share a meal
with those you think have no appeal,
with those you may despise with zeal.
Whom will you ask to share your food?

If you will learn to share your food
with those you usually exclude,
then prejudice may be subdued!
Whom will you ask to share your food?

19. Word Assassination

If others you with words abuse
and kindness toward them you refuse,
their lives with words you curse, berate,
your speech is only filled with hate.
You are then guilty of a crime—
assassination's paradigm:
assassinate those you don't like;
your words can wield a deadly strike.

Here's an example to despise,
where prejudice is no surprise.

Long-standing groups of children's aid
by Israel are now betrayed.
The children are from Palestine,
therefore this is the certain sign
these groups have terror on their mind—
They're "terrorists" Israelis find.
For "terrorists" they're but a front,
as Israel leads its own witch hunt.

20. The Domino Effect

We don't live in isolation;
    what we do affects someone.
What we say may be causation
    of a wrong another's done.

There can be no abdication
    of what we have said and done.
Both can be the incarnation
    of some evil, good begun.

Words can be our ruination,
    if we cannot curb our speech,
or can be a transformation
    and may heal a troubling breach.

Deeds can be our ruination,
    if they're rooted in conceit.
If they cause utter vexation,
    our lives will be bittersweet!

Section 3

Child Justice

21. To Be a Girl or Boy

Do you remember how it was—
        to be a girl or boy,
to have a chance to play all day.
        each moment to enjoy?

If so, you're not like many girls,
        and not like many boys,
who live in squalor, poverty,
        know little of life's joys.

Do you remember how it was—
        to have plenty to eat,
a filled lunch box you took to school
        and good shoes on your feet?

If so, you're not like many girls,
        and not like many boys,
who wake to hunger every day
        and never play with toys.

Do you remember how it was—
        to have good clothes to wear,
for summer some, for winter too
        you scarcely had a care?

If so, you're not like many girls,
        and not like many boys,
Sometimes there is no shirt or dress:
        for clothes, she/he rags employs.

22. Repairing Broken Children[1]

(Reflections on the US Border Crisis)

Americans, you need to hear
    a voice from your own past:
a slave transformed into a seer,
    with wisdom to hold fast.

It's better to build children strong,
    with boldness Douglass claims,
than to repair all of your wrong
    and all their broken aims.

A broken child will soon become
    a woman or a man.
Her life can surely be the sum
    of your immoral plan?

Have you no moral fiber left
    to help them with their needs?
Are you of decency bereft,
    while cruelty proceeds?

An infant child, a refugee,
    deserves a chance at life!
Take up responsibility!
    Yes, you can end the strife!

1. "It is easier to build strong children than to repair broken men" is often attributed to the abolitionist and statesman Frederick Douglass.

23. Children at Risk

Now rugged individualism,
    America's pioneer pride,
has run the gamut of its course
    with guns packed at one's side.

The open-carry laws invade
    the town and city streets;
no child is safe in any school,
    as safety one defeats.

In places now become renowned,
    the names we can't forget:
Aurora, Bolder, Columbine,
    where'll be the next gun threat?

Had I a child in school today
    I'm not sure what I'd do.
Homeschooling's an attractive choice;
    is this a choice for you?

For working parents it's no choice,
    their children go to school.
Their children must endure the risk,
    so who then is a fool?

The legislators are the fools
    who will not change the laws.
They do not care whose child is killed,
    their thinking's full of flaws.

Gun lobbyists risk children's lives;
    they want no new laws backed.
And children's blood is on their hands.
    This is a hard, cold fact.

24. A Child Alone

A child sits trembling all alone
    without a family or friend,
her face expressionless as stone.
    Will no one comfort lend?

As tears flow from her dark brown eyes,
    her mane of sleek, black hair
conceals the sound of sobs and cries.
    Six weeks she has been there.

Colombia is where she was born
    just six short years ago.
Her father from her life was torn,
    a street gang struck the blow.

They killed her father in the street,
    a gun shot through his head.
Her mother swept her off her feet,
    and hastily they fled.

For weeks, yes months, they trekked on foot
    and dreamed of a new start.
The mother knew they'd be hard put
    to follow their own heart.

They crossed a border, guards then came
    and took her mom away.
Then in a courtyard with wire frame
    they put the girl to stay.

Now there she's sitting all alone,
how sad this desperate scene.
Some lawmakers the scene condone:
How inhumane! How mean!

25. Guns

Availability's the key
whenever there's a big gun spree.

Were there no guns to shoot and kill,
how could one then with guns do ill?

OK, responds the NRA.
"You need a gun to win the day!

"You need a gun to kill the guy,
who wants to shoot you in the eye."

"Kill him," they say, "lest he kill you,"
that's the important thing to do.

It matters not that guns for all
are purchased at a nearby mall.

Guns are not bad! They are just there,
so, we can buy them anywhere.

Deprive a killer of a gun,
and half the battle has been won!

The other half means helping those,
whose posture violence might disclose!

26. Do Children Have a Chance?

Thursday came and went.
Nothing eventful occurred that day.
Then Friday came,
when our family gathers for dinner.
What a festive time we spent
with three generations of relatives
feasting on the best dishes
our mothers could cook:
fried chicken, home-grown veggies,
spiced leg of lamb with mint jelly,
deviled eggs, eggplant casserole,
rolls with edge-dripping butter,
and Aunt Jesse's fried apple pies,
my favorite! Absolutely scrumptious!

Just as I reached for one of them
I heard a loud pop outside
and a window pane shattered.
My sister, Jenny, sitting near the window
grew limp in her chair
and slowly her head fell to the table.
Mother rushed to her,
taking her head gently in her hands,
which soon were covered with blood.
Father ran to the window
to see a car speeding away.
Someone had randomly shot at our house,
and tragically the bullet struck Jenny.

My Aunt phoned 911
and EMS rushed to our house;
they desperately tried to revive Jenny,
but by the time they arrived at the hospital
she was gone! My sister was dead.
What dreams were shattered that night!
What love was lost!
She was only twelve years old
and so full of promise,
so filled with life and love;
her laughter was intoxicating.
That afternoon she had played Mozart
so beautifully at a piano recital
and received an award as
"Most Improved Student of the Year"!

Once again gun-violence
denied a child the chance
to pursue her gifts and talents
and to fulfill her dreams.
In a world ruled by guns
do children have a chance
to grow, to learn, to love,
to become adults?
Many do and many do not.
All children have a chance only
if we diminish the world of guns!

27. A Privileged Child?

If you were born a privileged child,
    and all your needs were met,
you never were deceived, beguiled,
    lived daily under threat,
then you'd live in a different sphere
    from children 'round the world,
whose daily lives are dark and drear
    and into conflict hurled.

You would not know the hunger pangs
    that gnaw at their insides,
or suffering at the hands of gangs
    and family suicides.
A baby yearns for mother's arms,
    but lies there all alone.
The sound of firing guns alarms;
    one hears the baby moan.

Such is the turmoil of the lives
    of thousands, yes, times ten.
Some grow up trained to kill with knives;
    at twelve they're fighting "men"!
If you were born a privileged child
    and never knew such threat,
let child injustice be reviled;
    it's time to pay this debt.

28. Evil Cares Not

The children played, stopped, turned around,
    the earth a bomb blast ripped;
they all lay prone upon the ground
    and of their garments stripped.

There were just six of them that day,
    four young girls, young boys two,
who'd gone outside a while to play,
    an hour before curfew.

Naked and still there dead they lay,
    but one struggled to move,
for only one survived that day,
    a fate one can't remove.

The hideous fate these children proved
    is: evil cares not who
from life, it will or has removed;
    it cares not that you're you.

Warmongers have a single goal:
    to conquer and oppress.
Five children's lives that day they stole,
    each parent's warm caress.

All those who foster hate and fear
    in children, take their lives,
deserve a strong rebuke, severe;
    no good from them survives.

It matters not culture or creed,
a Christian, Moslem, Jew,
each child from hatred must be freed
to live, to self be true.

29. A Refugee-Child's Plea

"With whom can I go play today
    without my mom or dad?
Without my siblings, who will say,
    'What fun'? That makes me sad!"

Someone says, "Here's paper and pen,
    and here are crayons too.
Outside the fence those big, tall men
    will all be friends to you."

"But I don't know them," I then said,
    "I know they don't know me."
One scoffed, "Don't worry, you'll be fed."
    "My mom I want to see!"

"I'm just a boy who's eight years old,
    my family's not in sight.
I'd like my mother's hand to hold,
    my dad to hold me tight.

"I dream of seeing them again,
    my family to be near.
It would remove some fear and pain,
    if they could just appear.

"The guards don't know the pain it's caused
    to tear us all apart.
I've shuddered, trembled, stuttered, paused!
    And yet, they say, 'Take heart!'"

"Take heart?" repeats the little boy.
   "Where are my mom and dad?
Where is my sister who's named Joy?
   I know they must be sad."

"Take heart!" you say. "Okay, I will,
   if that's not a wisecrack.
I pray you will my wish fulfill:
   O please, please bring them back."

30. A Freedom Coup

Would you a child to strife inure
    till that is all it knows?
Its daily task, endure, endure,
    as apathy just grows.

It knows not how to joke and play;
    it has no chance to laugh.
There's violence, bombing, every day,
    and streets filled with riffraff.

For children, who are refugees
    and find themselves detained,
are damaged slowly by degrees,
    their happiness restrained.

They've lost their parents in their flight,
    or guards took them away.
Without their touch it's fright on fright!
    Who can this fear allay?

The firmness of a father's hand,
    a mother's soft caress,
while now they by a chain fence stand,
    perhaps could lessen stress.

There is a future, don't forget!
    These children have one too!
Could they at some time be a threat
    when each one thinks of you?

31. Spoiled Angels[2]

An angel's what they first called him,
    just born minutes ago.
The chances for him first seemed grim;
    there was nowhere to go.
Nowhere to go to birth the child,
    no clinic to be found;
the mountains 'round were cold and wild.
    The mom lay on the ground.

Just then the village midwife came
    "Oh my! Your child is here."
"A boy," she said, "Have you a name?"
    she asked, as she drew near.
"Oh, yes! It's Juan," uttered the mom,
    as if it were a charm.
The midwife gathered leaves of palm
    and both lay safe from harm.

She wrapped the boy in a brown shawl;
    the mother helped with care.
The boy seemed healthy, though quite small,
    his dark green eyes were rare.

---

2. Poverty-stricken parents, whose poverty is often no fault of their own, want the best possible future for their children. It is hard for "law-abiding citizens" to grasp that human compassion is more important than mere observance of the law. To learn to think as poverty-stricken parents think about their children is an important perspective for all people who wish to be compassionate.

The mother kissed him on the cheek,
    caressed his tiny hands.
She spoke to him in mother-speak
    a mother understands.

"An angel," both the parents said
    "has come into our lives.
How can we see that he is fed,
    that he hardship survives?
Here all around are drugs and death;
    "no honest work is found.
There's marijuana, crack, and meth;
    the dealers wait around.

"For him we want a better life
    than we have ever had,
a life that's largely free of strife,
    where he knows good from bad.
We'll cross a border, break the law,
    if he is free of fear.
If he can learn from life to draw
    its best from year to year.

"We want for Juan to go to school,
    to learn and to be wise,
to know all people are not cruel,
    to live by truth not lies.
We're poor, we know, with little chance
    to help our son along,
but we're determined he'll advance,
    and fight against all wrong."

32. Too Late

Both rude and arrogant she was;
    her words were most unkind.
One wondered what could be the cause.
    What made her so inclined?

She rarely let another speak
    before she rudely spoke.
By no means would one call her meek,
    her habit was: provoke.

Her parents wondered: how could they
    make known their love and fear.
It seemed that each kind word they'd say
    was answered with a sneer.

Each day she wondered: Why don't they
    see *I* have teenage fears?
I'm so confused! What can I say?
    Will I just waste these years?

But when her parents passed away,
    she realized her fault.
Too late it was kind words to say;
    they lay within a vault.

33. Wishful Thinking

Some days I'd like to be a boy
    of eight just one more time,
at Christmas time with one new toy,
    when chocolate cost a dime.

At Christmas time with peace, goodwill,
    no racial wrong; no doubt;
but justice for the poor and ill
    we rarely sang about.

34. Knowledge and Reason

To learn, a gift beyond compare,
for every child should not be rare.
To learn builds each child's self-esteem.
As knowledge grows, each child can dream.
Through knowledge each child's mind expands,
each learns of cultures, other lands.
As children learn to write, add, read,
their mother tongue meets a new need.
They speak and they communicate;
they learn with others to relate.
They then can build community
and serve the cause of unity.
The education of each child
alone prevents a world defiled
by ignorance and thoughtlessness,
stupidity, and carelessness.
Through wisdom we search in the soul
for wisdom to make humans whole.

35. An International Language

I saw a child alone today,
but not a word I heard her say.
Her anguished muffled cries I heard;
they needed not a single word.

It matters not the tongue we speak,
we need not be a language geek
a child's sad cry to understand,
if we will heed the heart's command.

The heart says, "Listen, hear her cry,
for some will simply pass her by.
Embrace her with a loving arm,
so she will know you mean no harm."

In US border camps, they're heard,
these cries that need no spoken word.
They tell of saddened girls and boys,
oft parentless and robbed of joys.

Detained they are against their will;
too young are some to heed, "Be still."
All nurture need and health-filled care,
these surely the US can spare.

If not, the US risks a crime
and never will redeem the time.
Unless in Congress mercy rules,
our leaders show themselves as fools.

Section 4

Societal Justice

36. Vision of Humanity

What vision of humanity
 have current Christians, Muslims, Jews?
A vision of calamity,
 or one that care for all renews?

How fragile are relationships
 for those who solely look within,
and care for others would eclipse,
 as if their bias were built-in?

How interesting their sacred books
 reveal for humankind concern—
a series of suppliant looks
 for which earth's people all should yearn:

Care for the next, the next is near,
 let neighbor love be paramount!
Truth, honesty, respect revere,
 all hatred, prejudice discount!

These faiths were blessed through Abraham
 from whom each one of them descends.
What if, as humble as a lamb,
 they'd make with everyone amends?

They would be faithful to their past
 and to the present faithful too!
This kind of faithfulness will last,
 and humankind it will renew!

37. Civility

What happened to civility?
It vanished with humility.
If I think that stability
should mean agreeability
with every possibility
that fits my sensibility,
the likely probability
is heated volatility
and stark immutability.
One's crass inflexibility
can never have credulity.
One needs dependability:
sincere, kind amiability
to shun intractability
and create the ability
to speak with sensibility
and see the culpability
of one's own incivility.

38. Why not Compromise?

When politicians know they're right
    and know their adversaries wrong,
then compromise is not in sight,
    regardless if debates are long.

Some would not dare to use this word,
    for fear they would be seen as weak.
They make civility absurd;
    an ego's boost is all they seek.

Great statesmen know honor to gain,
    when compromise serves common good.
How sad the word's become arcane!
    The wise should show it's understood.

39. Complicity

Complicity's a blinding force
    in systems of society,
and often it's a subtle source
    of humankind's anxiety.

In systems of white privilege
    complicity makes unaware
that it's a human sacrilege
    to think in ways that are unfair.

Can we forsake complicity,
    accepting people as they are,
and honor all ethnicity
    in lands that are both near and far?

If so, we honor humankind
    as humankind deserves to be.
Though humans are not of like mind,
    they are one sole humanity!

40. Corona, Delta, Omicron

Corona, Delta, Omicron
are viruses fear's based upon.
Without a warning all three strike;
in this aspect they are alike.
Around the world the nations try
protective means while millions die.
Now disbelievers raise their voice:
"Protection is a foolish choice.
No mask, no vaccine, that's my right.
I want them both out of my sight."
But they can be a carrier,
that breaks down every barrier.
To claim a "right" that is a crime
could wind up murd'ring in due time.

41. George Floyd's Eight-Minute Death

Crowds gathered because of one man's death.
Police stood by at his last breath,
but one of them would not let go;
we saw it all on video.
Would not let go of George Floyd's neck;
no colleague held this cop in check.
Eight minutes George Floyd for life pled;
eight minutes passed and he was dead.

With protests, cities teemed with rage.
One asks, Is there not left one sage?
Is there no Martin Luther King?
Non-violence is a dead thing?
And while pandemic dangers rage,
America now sets the stage
for failed economy, health care;
for justice is there no one there?

42. Hospitality[3]

High on a mountain of Tibet,
    at least so I was told,
a village thrives one can't forget,
    that's very, very old.
Four faiths and cultures there survive
    for centuries side by side.
Their customs, worship still alive,
    respect their common guide.

They live by hospitality,
    the heart of all they do.
Aware of their mortality,
    they have a common view.
Each faith is held in high regard:
    The Muslims, Christians live
with Buddhists, Hindus, no one barred,
    each faith has much to give.

3. When I was a guest professor at the *Institut für Religionswissenschaft* of the Friedrich Wilhelm University of Bonn, Germany, the director, Dr. Hans Klimkeit, introduced me one day to two Christian pastors from the village mentioned above. He had met them when he, with another colleague, was one of the first westerners in the 1970s permitted to travel the famous Silk Road through Tibet. On that journey, he met these two gentlemen in their village and was deeply impressed by their story and that of the village. Both had become pastors after age sixty-five. They told the story of how these faith communities had lived harmoniously side by side for centuries with full respect for the other and told of how they celebrated religious holidays of one another each year. They explained that their primary scriptural motivation for this kind of life is the Bible verse, "You are the salt of the earth" (Matthew 5:13).

When major holidays come 'round,
        they have a common goal:
in one another's houses found,
        as if they were one soul,
one human soul to celebrate
        their joint humanity.
Their strong faiths do not dissipate
        to mere urbanity.

On that Tibetan mountaintop
        concealed from all to see
the world should for a moment stop
        to view how life could be.
In harmony to live as one
        humanity on earth
in a small village has been done!
        Can such life find new birth?

43. Ignorance We Can't Afford

In Africa parched, cracking ground
    has seen no rain for months on end,
and starving animals are found
    as hunger, drought, death's fate extend.

When nature's cycles are disturbed,
    that farmers know a harvest bring,
then violations go uncurbed
    from which the greenhouse gasses spring.

There's much too much of CO_2
    from fossil fuels constant use,
and fracking methods are a clue
    to excess methane gas abuse.

"Let science-data be ignored,"
    some politicians boldly say.
Such ignorance we can't afford,
    and nature's desperate needs betray.

44. Injustice

Injustice reigns in every age
    where leaders thrive on power.
Injustice goes from stage to stage,
    till anarchy is dour.

Injustice wrecks the human mind
    with ego-centered rule.
It seeks to rule all humankind
    with every selfish tool.

It robs the poor, supports the rich,
    the hungry gives no food.
Its every action has a hitch:
    work only for your good.

Can justice rise up to defend
    God-given human rights,
injustices and wrongs upend
    and rise to long-sought heights?

45. Intellectual Brain Drain

The intellectual brain drain
    Afghanistan endures,
results from war's horrific strain
    for which there are no cures.

The USA from history
    learned nothing, that is clear.
The Russians left in misery,
    the USA in fear.

The brightest minds wars oft destroy,
    or bright young minds will flee,
unless there is a Trojan ploy
    to lead to victory.

Alas, we've left Afghanistan
    in turmoil, disarray,
subjected to the Taliban,
    who intellect betray.

46. Learning from History

Democracy, autocracy,
    did we not learn from Rome?
Are we ruled by hypocrisy,
    politician's syndrome?

Did we not read of Rome's demise
    of truth traded for power?
With oligarchy on the rise,
    Rome's future was grave, dour.

With civil wars both lost and won
    then history's scene was set,
inviting Attila the Hun
    to victory! Don't forget!

Will we learn nothing from these facts—
    how falsehood crushes those
who undergird malicious acts
    that truth, justice oppose?

47. Love Is Why

We all are children of the dust
and earth to earth return we must.
How brief the length of our sojourn,
oft poor the things for which we yearn.
Each one of us for love is born,
and love we long for, night and morn.
No higher purpose can there be
than love for you and love for me.
But love must never isolate;
it is the guide how to relate
to each and every earth-born soul,
for love's our purpose, love's our goal.
No matter our ethnicity,
our calling is to charity.
Without it we defame the earth.
Without it we defy our birth.

48. One Race

What pity that our common sense
    betrays the common good,
if 'round our thoughts we build a fence
    and don't do as we should.
If we think we are always right
    and others must be wrong,
on humankind we are a blight,
    but to one race belong.

One race there is, the human race,
    with cultures manifold,
with varied thoughts that one can trace,
    ideas often bold.
Respect, however, there must be
    for one another's life,
for thoughts and language, sanctity,
    outrank both hate or strife.

For brothers, sisters all are we,
    the human race we are.
Our differences each one should see
    but not the other mar.
If others see in us a friend,
    someone who's filled with care,
our lives in friendship soon will blend:
    the human race's dare!

49. Thanksgiving

For what shall I give thanks this year?
    a question that I pose.
For whom shall I give thanks this year?
    Do you think my thanks shows?

Thanks*giving* prayers are full of words
    we often hear each year.
But are they much like sounds of birds
    we always like to hear?

Well-chosen words of thanks should stir
    in us the hope to serve,
not just the will long to confer,
    but show we have the nerve

to give the coats from off our backs
    to give the hungry food;
to do the simple, loving acts
    that replace ill with good.

Thanks*giving* is a powerful word,
    but how do we *give* thanks?
Make sure that *giving* we have heard,
    lest word-thanks seem but pranks.

50. Trust Reality

As bird migrations readjust
    and icebergs tend to melt away,
it is indeed with much disgust
    that climate change is in full sway.

As fossil fuels do their worst,
    the polar bears lose food and space.
Without help, they are surely cursed,
    and could it be they'll leave no trace?

And just because you do not see
    all this transpire before your eyes,
and do not trust reality,
    you'll know that truth like nature dies.

51. We Shall Overcome

As slaves in fields would often sing
      "I'll be alright someday,"
Charles Tindley[4] made this song take wing
      the gospel to convey.

"I'll overcome someday," he wrote,
      a hymn his church would sing;
its meaning by no means remote.
      They made the rafters ring!

This hymn would one day win acclaim,
      would champion civil rights.
"I'll overcome some day" became
      a vision of new heights.

The people soon transformed the song
      to "We shall overcome."
They sang it nights and all day long
      that Jim Crow would succumb,

succumb to justice and just laws,
      minorities protect,
for Black Lives Matter's a just cause,
      no person may neglect.

---

4. Charles Albert Tindley (1851–1933) was an African American Methodist minister and hymn writer in Philadelphia, PA.

Section 5

Governmental Justice

52. We Pledge Allegiance?[5]

Democracy stands at the edge
    of failure in this modern age.
What benefits a loyal pledge
    to liberty, when right-wing rage
opposes rights, justice for all,
    when compromise is a curse word,
and justice is a violent brawl,
    welfare for *all* is just absurd?

We pledge allegiance to a flag
    and to "one nation under God,"
but create then a giant snag,
    so others know the pledge is flawed.
Where's "Liberty . . . justice for all,"
    the last phrase that our forebears wrote?
Do they express our grave downfall?
    Should we refuse these words to quote?

5. US pledge of allegiance:
I pledge allegiance to the flag
of the United States of America
and to the republic for which it stands:
one nation under God
with liberty and justice for all.

53. Accountability

Accountability's the nerve,
    democracy's lone survival.
It justice only can preserve.
    For justice there is no rival?

No words can rival simple facts
    for which one is accountable.
In spite of truth-distracting acts,
    are falsehoods insurmountable?

Accountability takes strength,
    accountability fights wrong,
requires each one to strain at length
    for honesty and truth lifelong.

54. Another July 4th

On July 4th we celebrate,
    but what? is what I ask.
A nation born on wars of hate,
    should we in glory bask?

When European settlers came
    and crushed the native tribes,
for centuries they'd bear the shame,
    but who this view subscribes?

After the native tribes were crushed,
    the settlers then bought slaves.
Their cruelty could not be hushed,
    as wealth grew on their graves.

In World War 2 the US fought
    the Nazi war machine.
From *all* allegiance then was sought,
    forgetting where we'd been.

Although we all for freedom fought
    regardless of our race,
the racism that some were taught,
    was easy still to trace.

Today we reap what we have sown:
    division widely reigns,
and wealthy people so much own
    that poverty us stains.

A proud American I'd be,
    but first I must repent,
and rectify indignity
    and prejudice prevent.

55. Another Year

One starts again another year,
but constant is the fear on fear:
the hungry starve and children die,
and desperate parents ask, "Why? Why?"
There are still warlords in Sudan,
and Souleimani of Iran
the US killed with lethal speed
to satisfy an ego need:
to boast, "This makes the US great!"—
yet soldiers left to perilous fate.
While politicians fold their hands,
the wars rage on in Mid-East lands.
As Yemen wreaks of tragic war,
its children cry and ask, "What for?"
While Israel swallows Palestine,
its generals toast success with wine.
Is there no hope throughout the earth
that peace at last can have new birth?

56. Colonialization

Centuries ago explorers came
    from European lands
so their own nations might lay claim
    to land with their own hands.

They searched for riches and for gold
    and met the native folk.
Some wanted them to be controlled,
    but others of peace spoke.

Then settlers came from Europe's lands
    and claimed land as their own,
of native peoples made demands,
    attacks on them condoned.

France, England, Portugal, and Spain
    all vied for land control.
It mattered not the natives' pain,
    possession was their goal.

The settlers formed a government
    of colonies thirteen.
The natives' disempowerment
    is what this act would mean.

Some settlers, yes, injustice fled
    to find freedom and peace.
But in their quest the natives bled,
    injustice did not cease.

57. "Death to America"?

America, I ask, is death
    on your horizon near?
Your leaders strain with every breath
    to fill people with fear.
One president was reckless too
    in vulgar speech and acts.
Our nation's friends now us eschew
    for he broke our contracts.

This US president was Trump,
    elected though he was,
he made of Washington a sump,
    a joke of many laws.
Respect the office, he did not,
    for greed filled up his mind.
He thought success could just be bought
    and justice left behind.

Of Rome's demise, he had no thought,
    of history he knew not.
By it he'd not at all been taught;
    all history he forgot.
The masses were not on his mind—
    their needs, sufferings, and pain.
His ego was with greed combined,
    our nation's shameful stain.

We hear, "Death to America!"
    from nations filled with hate,
and it's not esoterica
    that Trump this did inflate
till nations, our own close allies,
    now question if our death
transpires before their very eyes—
    and freedom gasps for breath.

58. Destructive Addiction

Addiction one associates
    with alcohol and drugs.
But one addiction demonstrates
    it makes folk act like thugs.

Their self-addiction soon hijacks
    all honesty, respect,
and decency and truth attacks;
    all ethics it leaves wrecked.

The politician's self-ego,
    addiction quite supreme,
can care for others fast forego
    and steal one's self esteem.

This ego self-addiction can
    destroy democracy,
and there's no active treatment plan
    for this hypocrisy.

Without the conscience of the good
    that can be done for all,
there's little lasting hope that would
    prevent a land's downfall.

59. Evil

From evil, if there's no resolve
    to check its horrid ways,
the worst of motives can evolve
    that leave folk in a daze.

The theft of human rights is first,
    which evil acts subvert.
Control of others, a gross thirst,
    which human rights pervert.

In Russia, China, USA,
    in Israel, Palestine,
the wealthy seek to have their way:
    So, what is "yours" is "mine."

The rich disenfranchise the poor,
    the poor then poorer grows.
The right to vote is lost for sure
    where evil its face shows.

This modern slavery takes root
    in many modern lands
where justice cannot bear its fruit,
    because evil expands.

Abolish modern slavery
    and give all the same rights.
Without such strength and bravery,
    all justice has "last rites."

60. God Bless America?

"God bless America" is prayed,
    a plea of US heads of state.
It's sung where baseball games are played;
    Does it reflect a US fate?

Should God this fervent plea attend?
    What of the years of slavery,
and racism that has no end?
    Are these the signs of bravery?

To bless us should then God decide?
    Our forebears, yes, sought to be free,
but practiced dreadful genocide
    of Choctaw, Kiowa, Cherokee.

Some laws, imperfect though they are,
    have often fostered wrong, mistrust.
They've drawn strict lines some folk to bar
    from rights of whites, how wrong, unjust!

When of Pearl Harbor once we learned,
    though our own citizens they were,
we US Japanese interned
    and human kindness was a blur.

Dictators we've supported too,
    when our elected leaders kept
our economic wealth in view,
    a practice at which they're adept.

Why were our women forced to fight
    for rights to vote, a living wage?
Yet when oppression cleared their sight,
    they first were forced to bold outrage.

Today our nation doles out cash
    to nations that mistreat and harm.
How can our leaders be so brash
    and highest principles disarm?

Support for Israel we'll pay,
    even though extravagant the cost,
and Palestinians hold at bay,
    reminding them their cause is lost.

"God bless America," we pray.
    But we can with each other live,
if only we *sincerely* say,
    "O God, America forgive."

61. 9/11 Reflection

On 9/11 thousands died,
    a threat to our democracy.
But politicians that have lied
    are threats through their hypocrisy.

Perpetuating untruth, lies
    about elections and vaccines,
they're why democracy gasps, dies,
    shapes one of history's grave scenes.

One only needs to read of Rome
    and how prosperity gave way
to lies, life in a catacomb,
    and only ashes on display.

62. Insurrection

If insurrection is a word
Americans have newly heard,
that fears and anxiousness have stirred,
they know the word is not absurd.

As many ask, What can be done?
They hear the tales that have been spun
of January 6 that stun,
and yet democracy has won.

Was it a momentary win?
Recall, recall Hitler's Berlin:
Democracy must start again.
Wake up! Remember where we've been!

They died and gave to us the right
to freedom, everyone's birthright—
yes, natives, settlers, slaves ignite
the truth of freedom we recite.

63. Lust for Power

Why humans have a lust for power
    is not a mystery,
since human history is dour,
    and filled with misery.

For greed plagued humans from the start
    with Adam and with Eve.
And still it drives humans apart
    with goals but to deceive.

Deception rules our politics
    and often business deals.
It seems each party's bag of tricks
    dishonesty reveals.

Colonial powers year on year
    fought wars across the globe;
instilled in peoples fear on fear
    with every evil probe;

these probes their aims clearly define
    their goal is to destroy:
take forests, minerals, call them "mine"
    from Choctaw, Iroquois.

In Africa across the sea
    they captured folks for slaves;
though it may seem this could not be,
    soon crops grew on their graves.

And farther yet the Holy Land
 was desecrated too.
Colonial powers planned and planned
 this land then to accrue.

The evil that goes on today
 comes from abusive power,
attempts vast cultures to betray,
 their land, lives to devour.

64. Reclaim Democracy?

Reclaim democracy, but how?
What does the Congress want, allow?
Reclaim democracy, but how?
What do the people want, allow?
Reclaim democracy, speak truth:
example be for all our youth.
Reclaim democracy, act just,
eliminate hate and distrust.
Reclaim democracy, don't lie,
all falsehoods and all theft decry.
Reclaim democracy and make
accountable ev'ry mistake.
Reclaim democracy, admit
the wrongs that you, others commit.
Reclaim democracy, defy—
all prejudices bid goodbye.
Reclaim democracy be true;
accept those LGBTQ.
Reclaim democracy, root out
racism and all neighbor-drought.
Reclaim democracy and seek
just laws to shield the poor and weak.
Reclaim democracy, unlearn
injustice—now your main concern.
Reclaim democracy and be
a citizen who's just and free.
Reclaim democracy and trust
that citizens learn to be just!

65. The Death Penalty

Is justice—convict those who kill,
    because they killed someone?
Are we humane or inhumane
    to kill a daughter, son?

Is justice what courts execute:
    you take life, courts take yours?
The vengeance syndrome is acute,
    and vengeance has few cures.

Eye for an eye, tooth for a tooth,
    this ancient law lives on.
I've heard of this law from my youth;
    still folks to it are drawn.

Some folks' religion makes the claim
    that they should all forgive.
In spite of this most worthy aim,
    this is not how they live.

No one may claim simplicity,
    when one another kills.
The first thought is complicity,
    for death the public wills.

Some folks believe that God gives life
    to every human born.
But penalties by death are rife
    and life from one is shorn.

66. What if?

World diplomats all face today
    the multi-troubling task:
Will they look East, another way,
    West, South, or North? They ask.

Some western countries plead the cause
    of freedom, right or wrong;
some eastern countries now pass laws
    which freedom can't prolong.

The clash between the West and East
    asks, "Who opposes us?"
The US, China? Who's the beast?
    Old Russia, we call Russ?

This triangle of nation power,
    which dominates the world,
oft goodness, kindness both devour
    and violence is unfurled.

If West, East, South, and North all four
    resources would combine,
war, hunger, poverty deplore,
    all could with peace align.

67. Voting Rights

When leaders fail, where do we turn?
    The anarchists raise high their hands.
There's scarce a moment to discern;
    they devastate till nothing stands.

Then violence and fraud will reign,
    and justice is without a chance.
Integrity and fairness wane,
    and power mongers do their dance.

Is there a chance that voting rights
    can give to folk sufficient power
to raise a nation to new heights
    in what would seem its darkest hour?

This precious right some would deny
    to those who live in poverty,
or race can be the reason why;
    white-power would with this agree.

All human beings have the right
    to vote on their own destiny.
Those who reject this are a blight,
    committing a gross felony!

68. The Idea of America

America, why should God shed
    the grace divine on you?—
For slaves and natives you have bled,
    injustice through and through.

Of monuments to Lincoln, King
    we stalwartly are proud,
but native nations all would sing,
    if here stood Chief Red Cloud.

The idea of the USA
    did not begin with ease,
for freedom, justice went astray,
    which brings us to our knees.

The idea of America
    still struggles to come true.
Is it mere esoterica:
    just laws for me and you?

69. Long-Awaited Justice[6]

They waited some four hundred years,
    the Rappahannock Tribe,
a justice long, long in arrears;
    a joy no words describe.

Fones Cliff, the tribe's ancestral home
    is now returned at last.
This sacred place where eagles roam
    is theirs as in times past.

Oh, displaced Rappahannock Tribe,
    when settlers took your land,
your sorrow one cannot describe,
    when you from home were banned.

A portion of the land's returned
    to those who're still alive,
the sacred land for which they've yearned,
    four hundred sixty-five,

the number of acres received
    after four hundred years.
For centuries they were deceived
    in exile fraught with tears.

---

6. On April 1, 2022, it was announced by the US Department of the Interior that the Rappahannock Tribe of Virginia has re-acquired 465 acres of its sacred homeland area, namely at Fones Cliff on the Rappahannock River, an area rich in forests, wetlands, and waterways essential to bald eagles and diverse migratory wildlife.

But now where eagles nest and soar
   the tribal hearts rejoice.
Ancestral customs known before
   have now a living voice.

70. Autocracy

Autocracy's alive and well,
for autocrats the truth won't tell.
They say this word only to curse,
and how they rule is even worse!

Democracy they think's a joke;
they act just like an ole cowpoke,
who rides roughshod o'er all in view,
while shouting boldly, "That's not true!"

They lie and steal to have their way,
no honest soul can have a say.
Democracy cannot be whole,
when autocrats are in control!

Arise, all citizens, take charge!
These criminals are still at large.
Reclaim democracy for all,
or this republic's doomed to fall.

71. Meritocracy

The praise of meritocracy,
    some lend without reserve,
for it avoids hypocrisy:
    All, all new skills deserve.

Should nations then be relentless
    to shape a ruling class
by merit, or is this senseless
    as normative *en masse*?

"All may to highest wants aspire":
    a meritorious creed?
For some it seems worthy desire,
    but not for those in need.

The goal to educate, improve,
    and make for better skills
ignores the crying need for love,
    and help for feeble wills:

a merit system justice needs
    and charitable views:
if merit from wrong goals proceeds
    merit itself will lose.

72. Demise of Neutrality

Now here comes Sweden, Finland too
to join the countries of EU.
For years with staunch veracity
they've stood for strong neutrality.
And now with Russia on the move,
the west hopes this will safer prove.
It's courted both these neutral lands
with wide, wide open wooing hands.
For me, I like neutrality;
it often breeds civility.
So west, beware lest a divide
will mean civility has died.

Section 6

Apartheid & Justice

73. An Israeli Earthquake

What shatters nature? An earthquake,
which many creatures' lives may take.
It is not caused by malcontent,
for earthquakes never will lament.
It's part of a great natural force
without a predetermined course.

But humans shatter nature too,
and often creatures in their view.
And human earthquakes are like war,
for they know what destruction's for.
Attack at will out of mere greed,
or self-defend out of one's need.

In Israel there's an earthquake
that life and land both freely take,
where Palestinian families
endure each day such casualties.
In Israel this raging storm
takes on a furious earthquake form,

destroys all that lies in its path,
while thundering an earthquake's wrath.
It shakes the earth with weapons, bombs,
and leaves the children with no moms.
It creates desperate homelessness:
a Holy Land of hopelessness.

74. Children of Abraham

Three great religions plead for peace.
　　in land that's known as Palestine.
Yet hate and violence do not cease;
　　of peace and hope there is no sign.

The talk of many is a sham,
　　sincerity is a lost art.
How sad children of Abraham
　　their lives and others tear apart.

Children of Abraham, beware:
　　his children should the nations bless,
not foster gross, non-stop warfare.
　　Alas, they *must* now peace confess!

75. Palestinians Have No Rights![7]

"The Palestinians have no rights!"
    declares the state of Israel.
Against equality it fights.
    "Let Palestinians, go to hell,"
essentially it says to them.
    Destruction of your Silwan homes
will take place in Jerusalem,
    then each of you through rubble combs.

Thus ethnic cleansing's kept alive
    in Middle Eastern "Holy Land."
For purity Israelis strive.
    As Palestinians are banned
from homes in East Jerusalem
    where ancestors before them lived.
So home by home they now condemn
    as Palestinians are deceived.

---

7. August 15, 2021, was the date set to end the demolition freeze on sixteen homes in Silwan's Al Bustan neighborhood. Thereafter, the Israeli government destroyed these homes and expelled the Palestinian families. Israeli forces recently demolished the homes of the Ramah and Odeh families in the Bir Ayoub neighborhood of Silwan. Notification by the US Campaign for Palestinian Rights, PO Box 3609, Washington, DC 20027.

A Middle East "democracy"
    the nation Israel claims to be,
but it is sheer hypocrisy
    to honor exclusivity.
Democracy honors the whole,
    where all are equal in the state,
led by majority control.
    In Israel is it now too late?

76. Covid Apartheid

Though WHO[8] offers vaccines
  the Palestinians to protect.
Israelis say: *No, by no means,*
  WHO's offer we reject.

As occupiers they ignore
  their own responsibility,
and international law abhor.
  How inhumane can Israel be?

Refuse the Palestinian folk
  the necessary vaccine aid
will certainly Covid provoke,
  a grave injustice that won't fade.

The highest vaccination rate
  of nations now is Israel's claim.
What is the Palestinians' fate?
  More illness, death, more of the same.

8. WHO = World Health Organization.

77. Commandment Eight

"You shall not steal," Commandment Eight
    of the Commandments Ten,
but Israel, the state, can't wait
    to steal and steal again.

The so-called "Jewish Nation," known
    as Israel by name,
Commandment Eight denies, as shown,
    on Hebrew law brings shame.

While stealing Palestinian land,
    to which it has no right,
Commandment Eight Israel has banned
    and put it out of sight!

78. Vaccine Poverty

It's fine to learn some countries claim
    high Covid immunization,
distressing yet the lack of aim
    to help a poorer nation.

Bolivia, for example, has
    received not one vial of vaccine,
while nation Israel is known as
    a state success yet unforeseen.

Israelis this achievement boast
    while Palestinians few vaccines
now have from West Bank to the coast.
    How inhumane this must be seen!

Why must they be at such a loss
    when there is such a dire life threat?
Bolivia shares this heavy cross:
    where vaccine quotas are not met.

Will Israel and rich nations show
    concern for people without aid?
All human beings need to know
    that others' conscience can be swayed,

be swayed to help them in their need;
    that there are still in humankind
souls who, beyond all race and creed,
    believe their duty is assigned.

Their duty is to every soul
who's born upon this planet earth,
to share abundance to make whole
all lives from moments of their birth.

That's much too generous, some say,
Would Christians, Muslims, Jews object?—
"All persons must make their own way,"
a view that Jesus did reject.

There is a common care and bond,
a duty that we all must share.
We must to others' needs respond:
abundant life, a worldwide care.

79. Common Belief and Common Goal

As Blacks lament they live in fear,
  so Palestinians find this true.
One's skin's the basis year by year
  of what policing dares to do.

Are there no limits to the power
  officials of a state may wield,
whereby they poor and weak devour
  and to integrity won't yield,

believe in God's own power to care
  and reign o'er structures of the state?
The Bible, Torah, Quran share
  a faith that God will liberate,

will free oppressed folk from the state;
  even Palestinians and Blacks,
in spite of all the racial hate,
  and dignity that the state lacks.

These sacred books call to account
  the faithful to remind the state:
Justice for all is paramount;
  the call for justice cannot wait.

80. Defenseless Gaza

Defenseless Gaza, Israel knows
it can destroy with a few blows
of tanks, and bombs from its Air Force,
but it pursues a different course:
a few civilians kill each day
and try to keep Hamas at bay.
Just slowly starve and kill a few
so Gazans don't know what to do.
Deny them every human right,
keep human justice out of sight.
Destroy and maim a mother, child.
Make sure no one is reconciled.
All international law dismiss,
but know that Israel's fate is this:
Israel will reap what Israel sows,
just as Hitler's history shows.
The Holocaust can't justify
the rights of others to deny.

81. The Fate of Gaza

Loss of dignity to power,
a license lives to devour:
Israel the great and wise
sinks to depths one must despise:
"Gazans to our yoke submit,
lest your homes our bombs will hit."

Gazan children cannot smile
facing Israel's selfish guile.
God of faithful Abraham,
Gaza's made a paschal lamb,
to be killed at Israel's will
using lethal weapons' skill.

God of faithful Abraham,
God, who is the great I Am.
Palestinians and Jews
live with very different views:
"We're entitled to your land,"
say Israelis, "You are banned!"

Palestinians hear this said,
"It were better you are dead."
Long ago the forebears came,
Abraham, Isaac by name.
There were Arabs and Hebrews,
tilled the land as they did choose.

Enemies they weren't by choice,
till there rose a Zionist voice:
"God has given you the land,
stand up and the land demand.
Palestinians have no rights;
it is time for their last rites."

God of faithful Abraham,
your creation's not a sham.
All belong to humankind,
though all aren't of a like mind.
You created all to be
just one global family.

Help us rectify the harm
done by Israel with alarm.
Hear a Palestinian Jew
who of one solution knew:
faith, hope, love—these three abide,
love alone heals a divide.

82. Israeli *Kristallnachts*[9]

The terror of that *Kristallnacht*
    the world remembers still,
when Nazi-Jewish hatred shocked
    the Jews with threats to kill.

In Germany, Jews wore a star
    to mark them as a race
that Nazis Jews from all could bar,
    of them not leave a trace.

Attacking Palestinians now,
    Israeli's daily fare,
with Nazi-hatred keen know-how,
    Kristallnacht's daily dare.

Such horrid history to repeat,
    to act with Nazi rage:
this height of inhumane deceit
    in Israel's come of age.

9. *Kristallnacht* (or the night of broken glass) designates the time in November, 9–10, 1938, when the Nazis executed acts of violence against Jewish people in Germany and Austria.

83. Lifta

In Israel a village ghost
whose name is *Lifta* has no host.
Its Palestinian families
are one of the calamities
of war in nineteen forty-seven
when fam'lies from their homes were driven.
And though some houses still remain,
there's nothing can remove the pain,
for no one to them may return,
no matter how their hearts may yearn.
To make sure no one can live there
the roofs have holes beyond repair,
put there by the Israeli state
to seal the Palestinian fate:
homeless within their own homeland,
from their own homes they now are banned!
Don't worry, Israel has plans:
on *Lifta's* site with its own hands
to build homes of such luxury
there'll be no thought of history.
Still some cry out, "Preserve this place:
its ruins—a Palestinian grace."

84. One More Palestinian Orphan

He trembled as he walked away
    from earth turned inside out by bombs;
one shoeless foot caused him to sway;
    the purse he carried was his mom's.

She died amid the horrid blast—
    not one wall of their house remained.
A neighbor ran to him aghast,
    the young boy's clothes were all blood-stained.

Orphaned at eight, he stood alone;
    she took him in her warm embrace.
No one to say, "My son, my own."
    Of father, mother, was no trace.

His sisters, brothers too were killed;
    he searched, but no one could be seen.
The killers' goal was now fulfilled:
    to rid this land of the obscene.

Obscene, obscene, but who are they?
    Are we not all of humankind?
No one may say, "With them away!"
    Yet prejudice is well defined.

"Anti-Semitic!" yells a throng,
    but "Anti-Arab" never say,
or you are surely in the wrong.
    For prejudice both are OK.

To persecute a people's wrong,
    though they are different from you.
The humble, meek—they are the strong,
    this even Hebrew prophets knew.[10]

10. This simple truth Jesus knew as well: "Blessed are the meek, for they shall inherit the earth." (Matthew 5:5, KJV)

85. Water Injustice

Water, water, here and there
    but not a drop to drink!
An ever-threat'ning scare,
    so Palestinians think!

Water for crops, for livestock,
    to both it is denied,
like off'ring dreaded hemlock
    till crops, livestock have died.

Is there no water justice?
    It's needed to survive.
Israelis say, "Just trust us!
    You're lucky you're alive."

86. Silent Censorship

The subtlety of censorship
    sometimes we cannot see.
Indeed it can be gamesmanship,
    extreme the subtlety.

"Some sixty Palestinians dead,"
    the morning headline states.
But wait, is that all that I read?
    No more about their fates?

They just keeled over and were dead?
    There was no random cause?
Were they just found lifeless in bed?
    Should their deaths give us pause?

Yes, we must ask, How did they die,
    in prisons or at home?—
from gun shots, bombs? We don't know why,
    outside the golden dome[11]?

Yes, censorship is slyly smart
    in what it does not say!
It strikes truth at its very heart
    with silence every day.

11. The Al-Aqsa Mosque in Jerusalem.

87. When Israel Was in Egypt

"When Israel was in Egypt's land,[12]
    Lord, let my people go.
Oppressed so hard they could not stand,
    Lord, let my people go."

This is a universal cry,
    not Israel's alone.
Colonial slaves ready to die,
    sang thus life to bemoan.

From Holy Scripture comes this cry,
    and meant for all oppressed.
Oppressors, take note, by and by
    all those whom you've distressed

will rise up like a mighty band
    their liberty to claim.
And all of those who could not stand
    oppressors will defame.

Throughout the world oppressed folk are
    subdued by tyranny.
Even Israel like a Russian Czar
    designs conspiracy

12. Stanza 1 is adapted from the African American Spiritual "Go down, Moses."

against the Palestinian folk,
　　yet claims democracy;
allows its theft, death to invoke
　　through reigning tyranny.

If Palestinians now would sing,
　　this freedom-cry refrain,
would Israel now let freedom ring:
　　Let people go again?

As Israel was freed from harm,
　　in Egypt long ago,
will it with mercy now disarm,
　　let Palestinians go?

88. The Death of Shireen Abu Akleh

You cannot choose how you die,
    if you live in Palestine,
for Israel can justify
    your death with reasons benign.

Each day with camera well-armed,
    Shireen reported the facts.
Thus Israel was quite alarmed:
    each photo truth reenacts.

Abu Akleh shot in the face—
    Who shot her? an Israeli!
Does Israel have the guts to trace
    the evil it does daily?

Her murder happened in Jenin
    where Palestinians suffer;
an act despicable and mean,
    for which they have no buffer.

She sought to help those who are poor,
    those who have no human rights.
Without illusions of grandeur,
    she kept justice in her sights.

She sought the truth for Palestine:
    the rights of all to defend.
Her photos will remain a sign
    that occupation must end.

89. Moral Law?

Those who deny to others rights,
    are guilty of wrong by law.
Against such law Israel now fights,
    and moral law would withdraw.
Withdraw respect of others' rights.
      Who can such acts understand?
Immoral acts soar to new heights
    with theft of more West Bank land.

Without respect of others' rights
    a land is destined to fall.
As Zionists set their evil sights
    on Palestinians' downfall,
they lay the ground for their defeat.
      Remember the fall of Rome
when rulers ruled but by deceit,
    a ruler power-syndrome.

Yet at the heart of Israel's past
    are prophets of righteousness,
who spoke of justice that should last
    and overwhelm wickedness.
Indeed it is a fearful aim
    to ignore morality,
which brings on Israel such shame:
    stealing land so openly.

90. Masáfer Yatta[13]

Repurpose Palestinian land
 for military use—
Masáfer Yatta, there it's planned;
 there's no chance of a truce.

Turn farming land to firing zones,
 demolish local homes,
so all that's left is rubble, stones
 where military roams.

Already scores of residents,
 evicted live in tents,
evicted without evidence:
 ethnic cleansing events!

Meanwhile illegal settlements
 are built on West Bank land,
expressing Israel's sentiments:
 the Palestinians are banned!

13. This name designates a group of Palestinian villages (ca. nineteen) located between fourteen and twenty-four kilometers south of the city of Hebrew. The acute accent over the first "a" is added to indicate where the accent falls in the word.

91. Tolerance

Of those who may be here or there
    of different tongues, color of skin,
of different faith or kind of prayer
    an African or Bedouin,
"be tolerant," I've heard it said,
    but few there are who seem to be.
Will we learn this before we're dead?
    Is this so hard for you and me?

92. Who Are My Sisters and Brothers?

Let the Palestinians die,
    their land be confiscated.
The US need not ask Why? Why?
    Israel is compensated.

It's compensated by US
    tax dollars and the Congress.
As settlers West Bank land possess,
    US human rights profess.

The US policies a sham:
    say one thing, do another.
And does the US give a damn
    who is a sister, brother?

93. Peace of Jerusalem[14]

For peace pray for Jerusalem.
    May love your gates secure.
A constant sounding diadem
    of peace be your allure.

Who are Jerusalem's lovers,
    whose heritage they share?
What choir of saints o'er her hovers,
    Her source of constant prayer?

Since Christians, Muslims, also Jews,
    Jerusalem all love,
Today, each day it is not news—
    all hatred she's above.

Above revenge, the hate and fear
    we sense within her gates.
A holy city atmosphere—
    for peace, for peace she waits.

14. Psalm 122:6:
Pray for the peace of Jerusalem,
May they be secure who love you.

94. All We've Left Are Stones

Stones, stones, stones, all we've left are stones.
I thought, "These stones my family owns."
Our house of stones grandfather built.
What is the origin of the guilt
the state with shame has cast on him,
and which has made our lives so grim?
Last week the state sent a machine
to crush our house, an awful scene.
It turned our house to rubble, stones;
amid the rubble mother moans.
Stones, stones, stones, all we've left are stones.
A Palestinian family groans.